T0368490

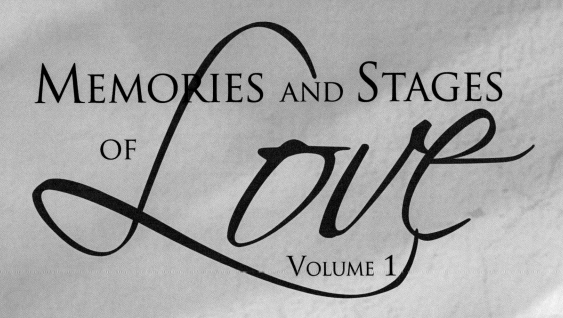

MEMORIES AND STAGES OF *Love*

VOLUME 1

RACQUEL VICTORIA SINGLETON

AuthorHouse™
1663 Liberty Drive
Bloomington, IN 47403
www.authorhouse.com
Phone: 833-262-8899

Because of the dynamic nature of the Internet, any web addresses or links contained in this book may have changed since publication and may no longer be valid. The views expressed in this work are solely those of the author and do not necessarily reflect the views of the publisher, and the publisher hereby disclaims any responsibility for them.

Any people depicted in stock imagery provided by Getty Images are models, and such images are being used for illustrative purposes only.
Certain stock imagery © Getty Images.

This book is printed on acid-free paper.

ISBN: 979-8-8230-2541-6 (sc)
ISBN: 979-8-8230-2542-3 (hc)
ISBN: 979-8-8230-2543-0 (e)

Library of Congress Control Number: 2024908076

Print information available on the last page.

Published by AuthorHouse 04/24/2024

authorHOUSE®

Introductions

My poems in this chapter are memories I've gathered together to tell a story and also teach a lesson on the many stages of love. Some are wonderful others have changed and taught me lifelong lessons and also open me up to step out and create a new me.

DEDICATIONS

Peace be still in your lives and forgiveness is the key.

To all my friends that hold a special place in my heart thank you. I want to say thank you for being my great muse in the creation and this chapter of my life. And special thanks to my true love you are amazing wonderful I love you dearly. I began with a salsa mix of love and longing for love and craving's that grow every time I pour my soul for love. Hear me with your heart and join me through this journey and hold on. You'll be blown over.

STAGES OF *Love*: YOUR EYES

I look into your eyes and I found my hope and strength I saw in your eyes my desired passion my ability to love intensely you've captured my soul with your song and my body sings every word of your great melody I look into your eyes I found my soil to sew my seed of clarity and peace. You've given me a world of ease and pleasant memories of love motion past and our sweet yesterday's oh how I love your eyes, I looked into your eyes for more time with you to express even more how much I love you, In your eyes I see what you see me your garden plant what you need. We're walking this road together called our life's journey and with each step we made it to thee other side.

I look into your eyes and watch as the hazel oceans sweeps me through the many storms in my mind. We dream together a future of unity and understanding our passion flow as.... I look into your eyes.

STAGES OF *Love*: WE WERE

We were walking toward each other then it seems as if we've walked through each other you become me I've become you, I've seen your history do you see my future. Time has held us in the grasp of its hand what seems to be a moment turns into for ever we were walking toward each other as the sun shined faintly in thee East wings of this blissful memories we gave into each other all of our hope and dreams, Could it be that you were meant for me or is this a familiar spirit. We were walking toward each other in the cool of the day and to my surprise you turned to me to say where have you been all my life as if we've never met. We were walking toward each other you reached for me, I reached for you we held on till we could no more then you went away for good, How can this be you and I we're just a dream in me or are we too souls that are lost within each other. We were a craving of Love.

STAGES OF *Love*: YOU FEED MY SOUL

I've opened up come on and rest yourself in my loving room, You add to my joy with love and understanding, I need you even more. Time is on our side cause we've willed it to be, baby, lover, friend you feed my soul, I've looked for you all my life and I have found you in the attic of my mind. I welcome you to live in the center of me and we will fill the basement of my soul, baby, sweetie, lover, friend. You feed my soul, We gather all that we have and all that we are and become one in the same as the years come and go on no one will we be able to tell you from me, lover, husband, best friend, you feed my soul.

STAGES OF *Love*: SHE NEEDED, FROM A MAN

She needed me to love her to wrap my arms around her she needed me to come see about her to kiss her on the cheek and tell her that she's wonderful and that I cannot breathe without her.

She needed me to say that she feeds my spirit with her eyes and her sweet smile, she needed, she needed, She needed me to calm her body with mine and tell her no worries I will take care of everything. She needed me to pour myself into her so that her and I became one then became us. She needed time with me to say how much she loves me. I know I love her she needed passion for her heart and to lift her spirits high even more She needed to know I'll never leave her for another because without her there is no room for even me she needed. I never gave her what she needed from me.

STAGES OF *Love*: WONDERFUL SOUL

I've waited to meet you by whole life. I never knew you were so wonderful the time we spent was like we were never a part. You were there for me, wrap your arms around me and I felt safe. Thank you for the time we shared and the love that keeps us together, My dear brother. I love you for my soul and peace of mind. So please remember me through your journey. I will keep you in my heart as I know you will do as well. Wonderful soul, I'll miss you every day. Say hello to mama.

STAGES OF *Love*: JOURNEY

The time has come to walk through this life with strength and understanding of what lies ahead The moments Have past catching hold of yesterday's mistakes and it's happy smiles of quiet joys.

This journey must come to an end for all But remember the laughs the smiles The love shared and even the sad times All of these memories give strength wisdom and true understanding that's what gives us hope and faith to overcome.

So as this journey continues Take the time to give of your self All that you have and every part of you, Make a lasting change and be a blessing to every one you met so that your journey will be remembered by all.

STAGES OF *Love*: A LOVERS FIST

How long will you sista endure a lovers fist across your head How long will you sista endure a lovers fist a blow to your back How long will you sista endure the pain and hate that he invokes upon your body the selfhatred in his soul for himself that invokes on you every time he feels the need to hurt and break your spirit even more how long will you my sista endure is it till death will you part and when you are dead will you my sista still endure.

STAGES OF *Love*: MR M D L

I know your name do you feel my face I can't be with you until you see me all of me Not just my hair not just my eyes not just my mouth or the way I say your name when you touch my spot I need you to know my hands and all the healing that I hold in side of me I need you to know my heart and all the love it was made for and craves every waking moment.

I need you to need the real me and not what others tell you of me I'm here open your eyes unlock the door to your heart Build your trust on my foundation and then only then will you see me.

STAGES OF LOVE: *Love* OH POWERFUL LOVE

Love oh powerful love I follow you just to get a glimpse of your face I go to bed yearning for your arms to be around me giving me the peace I know you have for me Love oh powerful love I've run after you screaming your name hoping you'll give me all of you I need you more than you'll ever know my heart has been broken so much I'm not sure if it's still there but when I see your essence My heart beats like it's the first time Love oh powerful love I've shadow your every move I want to know your every move I wish to move with you every wave you make every embrace you give every kiss when your presence began's a new you chameleon of you every grain of strength you deliver to everyone's life You've completely turned around for good.

Love oh powerful love Please hold me assure me that if I would wait a little longer You' ll be with me until the 12th of forever and I'll never have to feel the pain of brokenness ever again my life will be full complete and whole to know end Because of you Love love oh powerful love give me your clarity so that I'll see the real you in the face of the man meant for me and he'll say love oh powerful love I have found you.

Love oh powerful love I know your name and I've seen your face and I've reached for you expecting your passion to fall on me and flood my life with untold passion I want all you have and all that you are can I please know you for the rest of my life and when I am gone from this world Stay with me please love love oh powerful love take me with you wherever whenever I think about you so much If I could I would think of only you talk to me I want you close hold my hands hold my heart hold my life I am yours dear love oh powerful love my heart is open and my emotions are healed of past pains confusion no longer drags me down into obsession and crazy thoughts.

I am ready and very sure that I need you more than my next breath my arms hold a special place for you My life is for the better because of you and I'll never forget you nor will I leave you behind my dreams have come true cause you have breathed your timeless essence through me around me and you made a home in side of me Love oh powerful love our time is now and forever.

STAGES OF *Love*: HUMAN CHAMELEON

Let me be your human chameleon and I'll change to your color whatever you open That's what I'll reflect So whatever shade that is your soul the basement of your being I will become Keep no secrets and I won't tell you your lies I can see your true reflection and everything you say and do I am your human chameleon I will change to your color What ever your reflect That's what I'll become a mirror of you the real you not what you may pretend to be what you show to the world Hide not your eyes from me I will still feel your vibe for I've become you and rather you are near or far my essence hold my copies of you I love you and you know me now as well as you know yourself I am your human chameleon I am your every shade of blue gray and yellow as your mood changes It also changed me and we're flowing through thee forever motion that is you we're one you've allowed me in and I am so in love with you You add to the making of me You make me happy Let me be your human chameleon and I'll change to your color what ever you show That's what I'll reflect you.

STAGES OF *Love*: YOU AND I

You and I began our story in the middle of a storm in your life The kind of winds that blow away all sense of direction I am so lost inside of you and I You and I are tied to one another We can't let go The winds are higher but neither one of us wants to be the first to say goodbye We have failed I prayed for you to go away that things in your life will change without me But I just had a thought was my prayer nothing but a confusing Lie How do I explain myself I won't even try Why is the question you and I have asked with no sound answer you love me and I love you so I must ask where do we go from here you and I know we're in love but we simply can't push out of sight The storms in your life Could it be that they are keeping us afloat in the middle of your sky which is the meaning of you and I.

You and I after a long 15 year intermission We've come together again and the show is still going on you and I seem to need each other just to stay alive your breathing me and I'm breathing you as if we were one heart one being moving through this world as to souls in one body You and I began our story in the middle of the storm in your life you found me and placed your essence around me and I am at home inside of you and I'm changing to your shade your souls color and magic is our theme You and I share something so amazing and beyond our minds that when we sing our love song a sense of restoring began's and wholeness is birthed through us every time you and I are the perfect definition of a long lasting high You and I will never come down from We will never crash and burn cause you and I forever hold the flame of love passion and quiet joy.

You and I were made from a dream in that dream we are always making love to our favorite song how sweet it is to have you inside of me you and I were born to love one another Our lives were created for the moments of time that you and I spent in the center of me Again I must ask where do we go from here the storms in your life is trying to pull us apart I am unsure but I know I can't let you go won't let go You and I have made a promise till death do we part Can this really be true You need me as much as I need you Only time can tell how our story will end I believe you are more than my friend and you're not just my lover you are the other half of me.

You and I must go our own ways the time we've spent is now at it's end The storms in your life have overwhelmed me and overtaken you have we finally let go of you and I goodbye my love.

STAGES OF *Love*: DEAR LOVE OF MY LIFE

I wait calmly for you My heart flows in multibeat for the thought of you I love you and need you more than my next breath my body sings your song on a daily and your rhythm follows me throughout the day and your essence completes my dreams in my sleep.

Dear love of my life when I think of you I imagine your smile your touch and the feel of your hand I began to melt in the promise that I will see you and you know without a doubt that you're mine Together we will create a love that romance novels have never heard of but will seek form us because you and I define loves grand power and you and I mirror loves truth and loves greatest gift Dear love of my life as we speak Our love in the lives of our friends and family a powerful change will restore and comfort them all The grandness of our love will be written in history books for future generations must know of love that is you and I our love is a lesson in it self cause it was created before you and I were born so that when we blessed this world with our presence is when true love really began Dear love of my life I live love and breath for you I feel a sense of loss when you're gone from me So come home soon I just can't wait to see you I need you you are in important to me and I am thee amazing half of you.

Dear Love.

STAGES OF *Love*: IFP2

If you know that you know love is true for me inside of your soul then tell me If you want a life filled with goals and hope for a future already in place then follow me If you need healing and your heart is heavy and you know no other to bring or break you free Then come see me.

If you are lost and can't find a way through this maze called life reach for me and I will guide you to the other side of right and truth If honesty and a happy heart is what you crave and mind blowing sex of our dreams then lovingly put your hands on me.

If forever is what you see and can't live with out and you need some peace to give clarity turn to the left.

MY DEAR THAT WOULD BE ME.

STAGES OF *Love*: SWEET M M

I am saying goodbye This is so hard to write and even harder to say my need for you has changed and those feelings have called me to break the number one player rule I began needing you more than my next breath I made a big mistake I began to feel when you were near me I mean when you hug and held me I felt your soul whisper to me I would look to your face for the peace I'd always see when the world around me was driving me crazy.

When we had sex My body also craved food but the moment we were done I no longer hunger I feel so full I'm filled with you My mind and body held your essence even days after you had gone away I have told you when I think of you I would see you or hear from you well it's time that I say goodbye goodbye has never made me feel more sad right now And even more heartbroken.

Goodbye sweet sweet M M.

STAGES OF *Love*: I DON'T LOVE YOU

I don't love you but I need you like I need to breathe you make me so high I don't love you but I need you my eyes will lose their balance if I can't see you speak with you feel you Heartless you I don't love you but I need you like a summer day needs the sun just to be I don't love you but I need you it's a longing in side of me that craves every part of you.

I don't love you but I need you My body opens and my wounds are exposed The pain in the basement of my Soul screams loudly for you I need you How can this be you don't belong to me you belong to a lonely soul searching for thee essence of you and that's why I don't love you But sadly I still need you.

STAGES OF *Love*: WHAT I WILL DO FOR YOU

I will come apart for you I'll lay down my heart for you I'll make your dream come true I'll give you the moon I will take you across the sea I'll make you my King and if there is bondage in your life I'll set you free I will love you endlessly and when you are hurt I will heal you and hurt for you and when you feel angry and want to yell and fight I'll take your anger for you and fight that good fight for you and if you ever feel all hope is gone and you have to cry out take your hopelessness and I will cry for you I will be loyal to you for as long as you need me I'll give you peace I'll give you heaven I'll give you hope I'll give you time I'll give you me.

Stages of *Love*: Dear Men: If P1

If you want it talked about then put it on the table If you want it told to the world then throw it on the floor then put it in the trash like a used condom If you want it washed them take it around the corner if you want it when you want then don't come to my house If you want it taken care of and loved then take my hand If you wanted abuse turned inside out and turned upside down then put it 6 feet in the ground.

But if you want prosperity and hope love and peace Then comes see me.

STAGES OF *Love*: LOVE

You know that I need you I'll never turn my back on you cause without you I'm lost I'm not too proud to get on my knees for you to scream out your name and plead with you.

You've given me so much peace joy you've made me happy You are my one and only you give your life for me No one can give like you Hold me please so I can become the woman you want me to be I'll do what ever you say I have you in my eyes memory I'll never forget your face.

You make the pain and confusion go away from my screaming mind as far as the east is from the west you set me free Give me a chance to give my life for you hold you tell you every day that you're my only love and we can share the peace joy and happiness you bring to my soul Oh love.

STAGES OF *Love*: GOODBYE

I will always love you You are forever in my blood and every day I will breath you But I have to say goodbye I will always need you my heart will never forget your name and when I am dead and gone My body will still echo love in your honor.

I've got to say goodbye My mind is spent in thought of you when you're with me and even when you're gone I just can't take it anymore Your selfishness all of the lies have really gotten old My addiction to you Keeps me seeking your hands yours smell your voice I held inside my collection of you.

But I've got to say goodbye You and I were never meant to be Goodbye.

STAGES OF *Love*: HEART TRUE HEART

Be true to yourself heart true heart Give to you first honestly of the real you seek Be true to yourself heart true heart guard and protect your role in this life Tell all your name and take your place like a true queen.

Be true to yourself heart true heart share the fruit of your soul There are so many that are hungry for what God has given you Be true to yourself heart true heart always be grateful for what's been given to you and for the hell God brought you through never forget where you come from and remember to press forward to the wonder ahead.

Be true to yourself heart true heart let love and forgiveness be your number one rule sing your song of unity togetherness and call out to other true hearts.

STAGES OF *Love*: SUMMER WIND

The cool breeze of the summer brings calmness to my soul I am taking the time to enjoy this cool summer breeze looking out I see how the summer makes everything look so new and pretty I close my eyes and remember the time I've spent with you Also remembering how the cool summer breeze brought us close I watched the trees as the wind makes the leaves sway and flutter back and forth I am watching two birds search for food in the green grass still feeling the summer breeze flowing around me so cool and free The summer brings a wind that seems to calm the seas and waves and streams Summer wind a cooling breeze allows me to remember love that began in this season of summer could there ever be a time like this to began a new of everything including love Summer wind brings life and energy Oh how I love you and thee element that brings us together Summer wind.

STAGES OF *Love*: MEMORIES OF LOVE

Memories of you makes the light in the room open my soul for more of you to fill me with the love that had been waiting for me all my life This kind of love cares how my heart receives its entry into me This kind of love tells me don't fear I am here now I am for real now We will never oh how I've waited for love to say that to me I am ready for this kind of love that forever love that says yes I need you I am free to you We will be at peace in you.

Oh how I love you This kind of love fills the empty places I mean even the spaces in my mind that at one point had no meaning can now be at ease because of this kind of love I never knew my life could become complete with this kind of love Love listen I've got something to say love I wanted you since the day I was born and when you touched me for the first time I yearned for you love ever since the day you show me you are the most powerful thing and that you would share yourself with me oh How my need for you took over me never leave me for without you there is no me I found I would not be if it weren't for you Love love stay with me Put your arms around me reassure me that you will forever give yourself to me and I will do the same It's wonderful I mean beyond my mind and spirit knowing how great this kind of love really loves me.

Memories of love so sweet.

STAGES OF *Love*: LAST NIGHT

last night was mmm last night was so so sweet It was more than a good dream It was all that I need I can still feel you inside me You make me happy Last night as the rain hit the window pane I looked into your eyes and you said I love you I became filled with emotion and I held you closer to me We became one a part of your soul you gave me your mind your will and your emotions You said were mine again We are now one being our love has grown and it will hold us together as long as we hold on to one another.

Last night was mmmmm oh mmmm awawmmm lover Last night night was like a high I never knew I love you more than you'll ever know love you more than you'll ever know last night touched my soul so free I feel when I am with you Amazing the love you have shown me Lover of my life so sweet Are we at this moment in time can it be you were really meant for me.

Last night last night you were inside of me We made love So unreal It felt like a dream.

STAGES OF *Love*: THIS MORNING

I open my eyes and reach for you But you're not there was last night A subconscious vision were you really hear or did I fall into some ones dream that somehow connected to me or did I simply get lost in the essence of you some sort of mist that ruined the real dream that came before I saw you I feel alone and cold the morning has taken you away and I'm in love with the memory of you And last night never really happened or did it cause my body says yes you were here.

STAGES OF *Love*: SUGA DADDY

I met a man who said to me I want to love you love you till I can't love you no more I said sure sweet thang you can love me all you want Then I said but before you do that sexy boy Just tell me one thing he says sure mama What do you want to know I said baby Have you said this kind of thang before I mean it sounds like something I've heard before he says no baby you are the only one I mean you're the love of my life sweet mama let's make this happen I said Sure lover close your eyes and when he closed them I walked out the door you see I've seen this fool around the corner He had been saying those same old tired lines to the girl next door.

STAGES OF *Love*: LOVE IS WHAT I WANT

I love to love The love I want I feel it and love fills me with the love I want Give me the love in your heart Let me feel your wonder and your bliss for I love to love The love I want My soul craves you My body is incomplete majestic of you can it be I finally found the love I want and seek every moment of my living days My mind is consumed with you and I am open for you to come inside hear me deep within your center earth Let me in to root my creation of the garden that is love peace and wholeness I love to love The love I want and need so please be real with me Need me as much as I want you to let our story sing a new song I love to love The love I want.

STAGES OF *Love*: SOMEONE LIKE YOU

I've waited for you for a lifetime I never knew you could be so wonderful Now that you're here I can breathe I've never loved someone like you my dreams have come to pass My heart is full of you I will never let you go you've captured me Come walk with me into forever take my hand and I'll lead you to a love You never known we'll become one heart one mind two souls in one being.

I waited for you in the cool of the day the warmth of the sun in the arms of the midnight sky I waited for someone like you.

STAGES OF *Love*: SOUL IN THE BLACK

Your soul is black I can't see your face your voice is a distant memory Your soul is black an open void where you use to be I don't know you anymore What's your name?

I'm not your past experience I am an experience and one that should be wellkept Your soul is black Why did you lct it gct this way so lost so gone Don't let yourself hatred consume you oh well it's to late Your soul is black neverending fall down a bottomless pit of your own hopeless failure I can't help you No one can save you but yourself.

STAGES OF *Love*: MOMENTS IN LOVE

I look at you and remember those moments when you touched me with those hands I am remembering the time when I danced to your song Your music opens my soul We are now in those moments of love I'm remembering your smile and the way you looked at me So happy.

Times has chosen us for this love that is beginning for the now as our needs grow Moments those great moments of love you put your arms around me and I feel your power It lifts me I am so high cause of you My life overflows those moments of love.

The summer is warm the sun brings the lightness in your eyes to the center of me Oh how I long for those moments great moments in love I'm remembering the love love making we've done to no end The way you kiss my feet my legs my lips my thighs Oh how you send me through the winds of those moments wonderful moments in love My dreams are filled your passions The vibes you left in my bed and in my body oh how my body.

remembers those great and powerful moments in love Making love with you is all I want to do I love the way you love me love me for your soul I'll never ask for more than that I need you like I need to breath give life in those moments high high moments in love.

I'm remembering the day when you said I do that moment unforgettable moment in love showed the future of our dreams passion hopes and our quiet joys I love you.

Stages of *Love*: Moments in love P2

We have told each other that forever is what we've promised one another but we must start with the foundation which is love communication understanding trust loyalty and support These things are the strengths we need to stand together against any storm because the storms of life will always come we must talk to each other and not passed each other in order for both of us to be heard I want to support you and I will show you loyalty because that's what you need from me and you'll know without a doubt that I love you now what I need from you is love respect trust your truth and security And so if all is understood then our moments in love will take us both higher then any high ever created by man or woman Our moments in love will have no limits no cut backs and surely no layoffs and without question neither one of us has to be fired Another strength that will empower our moments in love is if my mind is always on you and your mind on me We will never part because I'll give you what you need you'll give me what I want moments in love takes away the stressor of life if we will yield and allow Moments in love should have our highest honor because it sets our souls free like no other moment in our living days Past or present Through our president can always change with in our moments in love.

CHAPTER 2

QUOTES ON LOVE, LIFE AND RELATIONSHIPS.

This chapter will give mini mind opening thoughts on love, life and relationships through thought provoking quotes, listen and learn.

1. LOVE, LIFE, AND RELATIONSHIPS

Illustrations by Nicole Pappas

Love quotes

Love is a challenge to see if you'll give all that you are with no questions. Love opens the soul and moves, in to heal and restore all that is broken. Love creates life, Which in turn gives birth to lasting relationships. Love is every shade of any amazing color yet to be created. Love life's up for soul gives life to the undead and brings together a lost family.

LOVE, LIFE AND RELATIONSHIPS

Illustrations by Nicole Pappas

LIFE

Life is a gift only given once. Life should be enjoyed and filled with love, and laughter with the promise of a new. Life gives hope understanding and changes that will always come.

Life holds a place for real creation and a chance to start again.

Life is a blessing.

Life spent in peace is richer, then money will ever be or will ever create.

LOVE, LIFE AND RELATIONSHIP

Illustrations by Nicole Pappas

45

RELATIONSHIPS QUOTES

A relationship is like a partnership all that are involved must do their part or failure will win.

Relationships can bring about change, good or bad. It's all a choice.

A strong spiritual life. Gives meaning to it. Relationship that can never be broken.

Honesty, fairness, and the divine spirit gives for ever hope and real understanding to a relationship.

A relationship between a man, any woman should be like royalty. There must be a sense of honor among the two at all time.

LOVE, LIFE AND RELATIONSHIP

Illustrations by Nicole Pappas

LOVE QUOTES

Love weathers every storm without fail. Love is the key to understanding your soul mate. love gives more of itself without complaining. Real love brings two lost souls together so that it may grow and repeat the same. Love can heal and renew a broken or lost heart. When given the chance. Give love all of you and love will give you more than you'll ever want and more.

Love, life, and relationship

Illustrations by Nicole Pappas

LIFE QUOTES

Honored life is enriched with peace, hope, and divine favor. Life has been created for a reason to change and create more life of grand possibility. Life can be longlived or brought to an end far too soon. Life changes are to make you stronger and move you closer to God's purpose. Life can be hard, sharp and piercing only if it's a chosen path, so choose the divine and favored the right way.

Life can open so much and close even more. Only time will tell. Life's spoken end

LOVE, LIFE AND RELATIONSHIP

Illustrations by Nicole Pappas

RELATIONSHIP QUOTES

Relationships must have rules not to hold back or keep bound, but to strengthen the foundation. Relationships give way to release hurts and secret failures, also to add and multiply through the power of the divine.

Give yourself soul to relationships that build and honor your greatest truth. Good relationships strengthen the soul. Enjoy each relationship that comes in your life, even if it's only for a season.

Relationships are meant to learn from and give your best, also to watch grow into something wonderful.

Love, life and relationships

Illustrations by Nicole Pappas

LOVE, QUOTES

Love is a gift given only to those whom's heart and soul are honestly open to receive its grand power.

Love should be enjoyed and shared.

Love is the most powerful force on earth.

Love is needed more than money, more than material things cause when we die, love will be the only gift we can take with us.

Love is prefect love is strength, love is divine power, love is hope for tomorrow.

Love, life and relationships

Illustrations by Nicole Pappas

LIFE QUOTES

Life is the grand divine favor of God.

Life was spoken into the earth and the earth came to be.

Life can be hard or easy depending on how we respond to it. Also, what is given in life, from conscious decisions.

Life calls for the attention of our conscious minds.

Life is as life does. Life can only produce what has been planted.

LOVE, LIFE AND RELATIONSHIPS

Illustrations by Nicole Pappas

RELATIONSHIPS QUOTE ,

Relationships are not oneway streets of selfishness.

Relationships are created through communication and true understanding.

Relationships cannot move forward without togetherness and likeminded thinking.

In a real relationship, both must be heard and understood or failure will overcome and end it all.

Relationships have the power to make or break. So choose . Each relationship through the divine power.

LOVE, LIFE AND RELATIONSHIPS

Illustrations by Nicole Pappas

LOVE, QUOTE

Love connects hearts and souls to heal and restore all that's been lost and dead. Love the honest and giving always multiplying its self.

LIFE

Life should be shared, nurtured and always in creation of a new tomorrow. Life should be lived in expectancy for the greatness from the divine. Relationships Relationship should never be onesided because it was never meant to be a oneway street.

Relationship should be built upon love, trust, honesty, and God's favor and grace.

CHAPTER 3

This chapter I'll give my own thoughts on different topics that I wonder about and give a lot of thought to like human behavior, love, relationships and life choices. Please enjoyed the trip through my mind.

Page 1. Human Behavior

Human behavior begins in early childhood in a sense. How an individual grew up, and how they were so raised. So many were raised by single mothers or fathers and others were raised by both parents and this all comes into play during the growth and development stages. Friends and the outside world also bring different personalities and so many ways of thinking. So when an individual becomes an adult. This is the sums of us all, and where we are in our present lives, our behavior and way of thinking can be changed by what we allow from family, friends, the world and whom we choose as a mate. I have learned. If you can't change your mind. You can't change your life. And it can go either good or bad, but it's all a choice, and mind set.

I believe lessons can be learned through pain and hard times because during those trying times when a way out is the main focus a solution is created and almost out of thin air. I have also learned what the mind thinks, on repeatedly will come to pass and also what's being said on a daily will also come to life by the power of words and a strong mind set. Meditation I believe gives a sense of clarity in it can free the mind of thoughts that may not produce positive fruit and creative change for all that will be affected. Human behavior. I have seen come apart by misplaced emotions the affects are mind blowing in ways that can not be fixed or corrected unless it is willed by the mind and then put to action.

There must be some form of action taken in order for the change to begin and a new mind set to stay in place and in practice.Human behavior changes over time. Some to a mature and wiser level and some for the worst. And, sadly, too many stay the same and never grow the beyond where it lies now or 10 years ago, Human behavior, I believe, is an amazing teacher and the rules are the same no matter how we've all tried to change them to fit our mind sets and personal needs.So, I believe having a plan and well thought out. Goals give us all something to look forward to with a positive mind and our behavior will follow action made in the direction toward those goals, plans and goals.I believe being wellbalanced can make a strong change in human behavior, but it is up to us as an individual to simply make the choice.

We all can come along in a more powerful way. By joining together with like minded standards and powerful purpose for positive change in our homes, our hearts, our communities, our governments, and this great country. It's through our behavior growth is truly born and developed into the greatness God has already put in place for us all.

PAGE 2: LOVE

Love I've come to believe is the most powerful force on earth and beyond. Love is so strong and amazing that when it's truly felt in its most pure form love blows the human mind to a place never known. Love is a constant giver and a multiplier, love is a producer and growth is the result every time. Love, real love is shown, I also believe, love must start from within. We can't truly and honestly love one another. If we can't or won't first love ourselves, Love. I believe must take root in the heart, and as the seed of love grows, it needs to be given attention every day, and all the time. I believe life can be so busy that, we as human beings don't give love our full attention everyday and all the time. So many have tried to live without love. And in the end have failed in more ways than one. I believe life can't move forward without love, Love is the driving force for positive personal change and community change. Love, I believe allows all of us to be ourselves without being sorry for being who we really are inside and out, So many have blamed love for their own failure and it is simply not love the problem that so many have fallen out of love with lovers, friends and even family. Because love never fails, Love I believe can change hardened hearts and give that peace that everyone seeks and desires all the time. Love is that powerful. Love, I believe, has its own rules and love's number one rule, I believe, is sacrifice of one's self for another to give more of your self is to truly love someone else. Love is not some long lost secret love is an open book so that all may come and gather their part and in turn give love away. Love is a constant healer, a healer of hearts,minds, live, and family. Love by no means cauese pain, rejection, or confusion, For that matter.

Love will last till the end of time and beyond this world. Love is God's divine favor for our lives and the foundation for all beginning, Love, gives, so much strength to come through and overcome, Love is an artistic expression of the heart and soul. Also, love is freedom from past hurts and wrong turns in this journey of life. Love is showing compassion to whom it is due and that is all that are in need of a little love and compassion. I believe love is constantly giving birth to its self and love shows us we can do the same in love majestic strength constantly giving birth of the greatness in us For the growth of others. In love all things are possible. I believe love can change the wrong being done in this world, but it has to be a joint decision among everyone time will tell the story, But then again, time is very short, so now would be the best time to walk in the every day newness of love and continue to give love every day with all heart.

PAGE 3: RELATIONSHIPS

Relationships can be amazing connections among families, siblings, lovers, and friends. I also believe that relationships take a lot of work on everyone's part, not just one person, but everyone involved, Relationships, come different forms and can also bring different levels of joy. For example, the relationship between mother and child is like no other, and the joy a mother feels when she sees her child's face for the first time the joy that brings can never be replaced by any other joy. Also falling in love for the first time is another amazing way to see and feel the power of love in a relationship. This kind of love is a majestic feeling and it makes one feel like their on top of the world, and one can feel like they will never come down from that high emotion of what they feel is true love.

- Relationships can be a living thread that breathes life into the world and creates growth. There are people that come into your life for a reason, and there are some that come into your life for a season. I believe all connections happen to bring about a great change, also give a powerful lesson. Relationships can be hard if allowed it is a choice and sometimes a hard one to make. Relationships can feel like a prison when the one you love don't love them sleves his or her love can be very hurtful ways. For example, a lovers fist. This can be his or her way of showing what they believe is love and what that does is create more hurt and confusion. True love never hurts nor is it painful and confusing. Time is a powerful tool in learning someone's life story before beginning a relationship. Relationships have their ups and downs but it's when we work together as a team as lovers as family and best friends, is when we are truly in a strong and powerful meant to be,In Relationship I believe that honesty, communication, can strengthen relationships and bring everyone involved a lot closer. Now sometimes too much honesty can be too much for some to handle. For example, a wife always telling her husband what's on her mind. Some call it giving him a piece of her mind, but that's just it. Never give just a piece of any part of your self. It's either all or nothing at all. Relationships are our foundation to greatness and emotional health, and also you get what you give out of each relationship. Again, it's what we choose to have in our lives and what we just don't want in a relationship, Be it a parent, friends, lovers, best friends, and even extended families. So choose wisely in what with whom you want to build a relationship cause you'll never know what you are going to get . So you know what you truly want in a relationship.

PAGE 1: LIFE CHOICES

I believe everything in life is a choice, I mean, we all can choose to be happy, sad, angry, hopeful, crazy, honest, and at peace with our lives, our family and friends. Also, I believe everything is a choice. I choose to be happy, loved, powerful and I choose peace of mind. I will say so many things in life can happen and it seems it was out of one's own choosing but choosing, but it was a seed that was planted in days past that calls to the problem of today. I will also say that some chooses can be very hard to make. For example, a man choosing how to spend his time with his elderly mother and his woman and or wife he loves them both deeply. But again, the choice is very hard to make, but it must be done.

I believe having patience is a choice and can also be very hard to choose. There are so many things in life we must wait on, for example, a woman is so in love and always wanting to be with the man, but she must remember there are other responsibilities that must be given his undivided attention as well, so patience must be her focus and a strong source of comfort. I didn't say it will be easy but I am saying it's a choice.

Life has its many faces and so do the people in your life, and sometimes the changes in those relationships can cause those known faces to change. For example, in friendships, one or more can be going in the same direction, like from high school to college, but one friend could choose to quit school to start a family and the other friends can choose to go down the same world, but then turn the different direction now. At one point in life. The friendship was strong, but because of the different choices. The friendships can break apart forever. So at this point in time, both or all that are involve having to make their mind up where do we all go from here and can the friendship be strong again. Or were those relationships, just for a season.

Again, I must say it is a choice, we can all choose our own lives by what we will allow to help or control our lives, choices. So I say in closing choose love, friends, soul mate, happiness, joy, and more importantly, choose God, peace of mind and self love, patience with those who are in your life that you have chosen to., Always put God first in all, life choices.

Printed in the United States
by Baker & Taylor Publisher Services